Be Filled with
Faith

Blue Mountain Arts®

Be Filled with
Faith

*Words of Well-Being
to Strengthen Your Spirit*

Rachel Snyder

Blue Mountain Press™
Boulder, Colorado

Library of Congress Catalog Card Number: 2009043300
ISBN: 978-1-59842-473-7

◼ and Blue Mountain Press are registered in U.S. Patent and Trademark Office.
Certain trademarks are used under license.

Printed in China.
Second Printing: 2011

✪ This book is printed on recycled paper.

This book is printed on paper that has been specially produced to be acid free (neutral pH) and contains no
groundwood or unbleached pulp. It conforms with the requirements of the American National Standards
Institute, Inc., so as to ensure that this book will last and be enjoyed by future generations.

Library of Congress Cataloging-in-Publication Data

Snyder, Rachel.
 Be filled with faith : words of well-being to strengthen your spirit / Rachel Snyder.
   p. cm.
 ISBN: 978-1-59842-473-7 (trade pbk. : alk. paper) 1. Faith—Meditations. I. Title.

 BL626.3.S69 2010
 242—dc22

                                                                              2009043300

Blue Mountain Arts, Inc.
P.O. Box 4549, Boulder, Colorado 80306

Contents

Introduction

Faith is a precious commodity that money can't buy. It must be cultivated from within—nurtured by an open heart and lifted up by a willing spirit. Faith won't suddenly show up on your doorstep one day, but when you prepare the way for faith, you may be astonished at the inner strength that becomes yours. You'll feel more empowered—better able to navigate life's unexpected twists and turns with less stress and a greater sense of peace.

From strong spirit, strong faith is born. When you are filled with faith, you may find yourself being patient, awestruck, and unafraid of your fears. You may be humble, bold, connected, forgiving, and exactly who you are. Your faith will express itself in ways seen and unseen by those around you, and you may even surprise yourself. Most importantly, you will discover an endless source of support that can carry you through times of great challenge as well as great joy.

The words of well-being on these pages will inspire, comfort, and guide you to greater spiritual strength and the faith that accompanies it. Savor each word, and take in what resonates with you most. Read the pages from front to back, or skip around as your spirit leads you. Any way you choose to engage with these words is the right way for you.

May you be filled with faith today and always.

— Rachel Snyder

Be Open

Faith will not pound on your door demanding to be let in. You must open your heart and do what you can to offer a most inviting invitation. When you allow yourself to be open, you tear down the walls that have kept you locked up in fear or despair. You fling open the gates and windows that have rusted shut. This tells faith that you are ready to embrace her with a hearty welcome, that you're open to change in your life, that you want things richer and more satisfying, and that the old ways aren't really working for you anymore. Let faith know that there's a place for her in your days and nights and that you are prepared to believe in things unseen and remarkable. Let yourself stretch through the discomfort and into a place of greater openness. When you least expect it, when you're not looking, the moment will come: faith will slip quietly over the threshold without knocking and take up residence deep inside, in a room you have created just for her.

Be Present

How can faith find you if you are not fully present? Every moment offers you the opportunity to concentrate on what's right in front of you, to bring all your attention to the matter at hand, to focus on the person sitting across the table. When you are here, now, faith will land at your side. However, if your body is in one place and your thoughts in another, any attempt at authentic experience is likely to slip through your fingers. If you are spinning this way and that, hovering just above the ground, dizzy with indecision and distracted by discord, faith will elude you. Remember: This moment will never return. This precise set of internal and external factors will never again intersect. Zero in on the moment. Acknowledge and accept all that it offers you. Frantic multitasking might allow you to get certain jobs done—but it will not support efforts to enliven your spirit and create a well-tempered life.

Be Patient

As much as you want things when you want them, life will not always proceed according to your personal schedule. Patience makes the wait easier. There is a timetable beyond your reach, and no amount of pushing and prodding, hoping and wishing, will make a difference. Instead of focusing a laser beam on the objects of your desire, can you have faith in the slow unfolding? Life doesn't always flow in a straight line, and along the byways and curves, peaks and valleys, lay pockets of peace. When you come upon one, allow yourself to pause and trust that all is well and moving forward. Even as chaos and flux surround you, you may choose to read an uplifting book, listen to soothing music, take a walk in nature, or curl up for a nap. Why not relax a bit and let things take their course? The work of life goes on at its own speed, with or without us, and sometimes it's best to get out of the way.

Be Your Own Experience

Ultimately, all you have is your own experience. You can read about others' experiences, watch them move past you on the big screen, or observe them up close and personal. But all you'll ever truly know, like you know the back of your hand, is what you personally experience. What does it matter what the experts say if you experience something altogether different? How can you subscribe to conventional wisdom when your own inner wisdom cries out a different tune? If you think you're supposed to be joyful, yet you feel a huge hole in the pit of your being, what will you embrace? As you venture out into your walk of faith, you can try on a closetful of identities only to find that few of them fit. When you find the path that is yours alone, it will hug you like a glove and last throughout your lifetime. When all is said and done, all you can rely on is your own experience, and trust that others will rely on theirs.

Be Optimistic

Negative thinking and a cynical attitude will only lead to more of the same. Why choose to create a downtrodden, "poor me" view of the world? Staying positive requires more than hollow words and cheery clichés. Instead, make a conscious choice to see the good and true in every situation. Change your thinking and see the blessing instead of the curse, the opportunity instead of the obstacle, the opening of something new and better rather than the dismal same old, same old. Be the bearer of good news, not the one who circulates the snarky and sarcastic. Remind others that things will get better—even if they first worsen for a while—and remind yourself of the same. Every thought has the power to become reality, just as every seed carries the potential to flower. Whether you stew in your juices of resentment and fear or surround yourself with a savory blend of the positive and upbeat is your choice. Choose wisely: be optimistic.

Be Empty

In the rush to fill up every emptiness and hunger in your life, consider that "empty" can be a rich and satisfying place. If you fill up every moment with distractions, with busywork, with shopping for items you don't need, with people who only create the illusion of authentic friendship, you will never experience the fruitfulness that "empty" can bring. "Empty" is where new life is created; it's the void from which all things are born and the teapot we can refill with our contents of choice. Your empty feelings will not last forever because nature abhors a vacuum, and fresh beginnings will always take root eventually. This can be scary and unfamiliar, yet if you allow yourself to touch the face of emptiness, even for a short while, a rich fullness will follow in time. Remember that even when a blazing wildfire destroys a lush forest, it is only a matter of time before fresh growth begins to regenerate life and renew the beauty of the woods.

Be Awake

It's all too easy to sleepwalk your way through life. You adhere religiously to a daily or weekly schedule, go through the same motions, continue spinning the same wheels—all while in a vaguely hypnotic state of being. Life continually offers you wake-up calls, yet time and again, you roll over, hit the snooze button, and choose to ignore them. Might there be more to life than this? Is it possible that there are facets to your existence that you have never considered? Open your eyes and gaze in another direction. Awaken from your past and venture into a new future. Brush the sleep from your eyes and vow to see people, places, and possibilities in extraordinary ways. Walking through your days and nights numbed to genuine experience may feel safe and familiar, but it can prevent you from actively engaging in an entire universe whose only desire is for you to arise to greater freedom, happiness, and joy.

Be Searching

Being open to faith doesn't mean you're closed off to other avenues. As your spirit strengthens, it expands. As you probe your inner depths more freely, your outer life develops in surprising ways. For most of us, faith is not an absolute. Sometimes you will waver, and that's all right. Sometimes you will have questions, and that's all right, too. Faith doesn't want you to stop looking and asking and exploring new frontiers. Each time you bump up against uncertainty, you have the opportunity to revisit your intentions and recommit yourself to the journey that is yours alone. Don't expect one day to know all the answers to all your questions. It is the searching and asking and wondering that enrich your experience as you put one foot in front of the other. The shortest distance between two points is a straight line, but the abundant, spirited life is discovered through meandering side trips and so-called detours that yield unexpected discoveries. You can eventually uncover what you're searching for, though it may not always be precisely what you believe you set out to find.

Be Available for Grace

Not every moment of your life is a direct result of cause and effect. Sometimes you experience something that seems inexplicable—as if you were chosen to receive a gift you did not order. After a lifetime of never winning, never being showered with good fortune, never feeling the gold ring touch your hand, grace enters your life and serves up a taste of the rare and wonderful. It can be as small as finding a crisp dollar bill on the grass or as fleeting and precious as being the first to greet a newborn or step across freshly fallen snow. You may think it's your lucky day, though something deeper is at work. If you release your old beliefs that nothing good ever comes your way, grace will find you and reward you in ways large and small. She's always close by, looking for chinks in your armor and waiting to see if you will soften your stance enough to believe you are worthy. Grace knows without question that you are, and if you let her, she's prepared to prove it.

Be Balanced

No matter how devoted you are to your spiritual growth, someone still needs to wash the dishes and feed the cat. Your best course is to keep both feet firmly planted, even as you explore your personal heaven. Your spiritual pursuits are strengthened when you remain grounded. Faith exerts her greatest power when you meet her halfway with tools in hand. Focusing exclusively in any one direction will throw you out of balance, as though attempting to drive on only three wheels. The ride will be rough and real progress negligible. There's no rigid formula you must follow. You might dedicate one weekend to clearing clutter out of the garage and the next to releasing the emotional clutter surrounding unresolved childhood issues. Some days you will tend to mental tasks, and other days you may be inspired to minister to the affairs of your body, heart, or spirit. You are a finely tuned organism with interwoven elements that cannot be separated. Keeping an even keel supports harmony and wholeness in your life, regardless of what storms may rage around you.

Be Expectant

What if miracles and synchronistic blessings were everyday occurrences? How would your outlook change, your demeanor shift, if you fully expected that something wonderful awaited you around every corner? Could you imagine expecting that every phone call will be a harbinger of delicious news or upbeat support? What if you anticipated that every person you meet will look you in the eye and greet you with a smile? Once you routinely expect good fortune and uplifting experiences, you will find them more plentiful than you ever could have expected. What expectations will you carry? You can expect a miracle, a touch of grace, a kindness sent your way, a moment of sweetness. You can choose to expect prosperity in all facets of your life. And if these fruits do not appear right away, you can choose to expect that the time is not quite right and they are on the way. The grandest outcomes are indeed born out of your greatest expectations. Expectancy brings new beginnings and renewed hope in all that is yet to be.

Be Willing

Faith seeks out the willing. If you are sincerely willing to bring greater faith into your life, half the battle is won. You can signal your willingness by acknowledging that there is someone or something larger and wiser than yourself and then allowing that force to lead the way. If you are willing to release your hold on timeworn resentments and anger, faith will help carry them away. If you are willing to accept the inner doubts and judgments that fill your mind and recognize that they are part of who you are, faith will help you replace them with self-loving thoughts designed to ease your way. Faith makes no demands and issues no ultimatums, but rather invites you to be willing to cry and laugh, to rise up and collapse, to be bold and vulnerable, and to accept that discouragement and uncertainty are part of the journey you have agreed to take. Faith is not a taskmaster who insists that you struggle through an arduous and endless voyage. What is expected above all is that you show you are willing.

Be Thoughtful

When you seek to live from a greater place of heart and spirit, you don't stop being thoughtful. What may change, however, is that the incessant thinking, rethinking, overthinking, and analysis of every detail of your life will slow down and eventually cease. Thoughtfulness asks you to pause for a moment, to ponder the action you're about to take, and to feel with certainty that the thought and the action that follow are in synch with each other. When your thoughts are rooted in forgiveness, generosity, serenity, and the greatest good for all involved, they are most likely to bear results of a similar vein. Take a look before you leap. Clarify your intention before you speak. There's no need to endlessly rehash the inklings that arise through your gut feelings. It takes but a moment to ascertain if you are being thoughtful. In time, you'll harness the ability to feel it, know it, and follow through with actions that reflect your thoughtfulness.

Be Passionate

A strong spirit is built on a foundation of passion. Surely there is one need or one cause in the world that fires you up like no other and compels you to action. Pay attention to how you feel when you read an article, listen to a radio broadcast, or watch a program that illuminates human, animal, or environmental suffering. These injustices will feel so inherently wrong, so intolerable, that it will be impossible for you to sit idly by while they continue. You might feel angry, frustrated, tearful, nervous, or raring to go. Your passion is fuel for action. Your job is not to save the world or even to save one person. Your assignment is to acknowledge the enthusiasm and energy flowing through your body and to channel it into good deeds—large or small, across the street or around the world. Passion fills you with eager excitement and newfound vigor. Look around you at the people who glow with life and health and an indefinable sense of being alive. Chances are good they've discovered their passion.

Be Able to Say "No"

If you say "Yes" to every request for your time, your heart, and your mind, where is there room for faith to enter? There are twenty-four hours in every day—time enough for those activities that wholly nurture your spirit, but only if you have thoughtfully declined the lesser demands pulling at you from all directions. For your own well-being, you must cultivate the ability to say "No." Others may be disappointed or even angry, yet it is not your job to please everyone all the time. Saying "Yes" under pressure or in the face of flattery, guilt, or fear of retribution is unlikely to strengthen your spirit. To the contrary, your calendar will be chock-full and your candles will burn at both ends while your inner reserves dwindle and sputter. Learning kind yet definitive ways to say "No, thank you" is as important as learning to say "I love you." The only difference is that this time you declare those three important little words out of love for yourself. What's more, when you say "No," it opens the door for someone else to proclaim a wholehearted "Yes."

Be Loving

It's not easy to love everyone all the time—or even to love some people at all. Perhaps, though, you can give it a try. Perhaps you can discover something to love in a person who seems totally unlovable. Has that person made an effort in good faith, only to fall short of the goal time and again? Has the situation worsened despite all good intentions? Might that person be tormented by inner demons that you simply will never be able to understand? When the mind presents you with innumerable reasons not to love, it may be time for the heart to step forward and take center stage and do exactly the opposite. You can be loving toward others without inviting them home, spending long hours with them, or talking endlessly about love. Loving just is. You feel it, you carry it close, and you express it in kind, compassionate ways. A beautiful thing happens when you choose to be loving: all of a sudden, you feel that much more loved.

Be Tenacious

In the midst of your toughest days and nights, precisely when you feel you cannot possibly dredge up another iota of inner strength, life will insist that you steadfastly persevere. You will face an issue that matters deeply and requires sinking your teeth in and not letting go. During these challenges, faith deserves more from you than a fleeting thought or a passing glance. When it truly matters most, you must call up an unwavering commitment to maintain your bearings and stay the course. You must neither give up nor give in. At the same time, however, you may allow yourself to surrender to a greater force within you. Tenacity arises from a place of strength and deep knowing; it is an altogether different quality than desperate grasping or bullheaded stubbornness. When the cause is just and your instincts are rooted in the pursuit of truth and goodness, your determination will fill you with an unshakable will to outlast the trials at hand.

Be Humble

Arrogance, pride, self-righteousness, and an overblown sense of self do not offer a fertile environment in which faith can thrive. Remember that you are human, and be humble. Remember that the richness of life is measured in how many hearts you touch along the way and how often you allow yourself to be touched by others. Acknowledge and embrace your flaws, your weaknesses, and your mistakes, and know that you still hold a unique place in an immense and magnificent whole. You need not draw attention to yourself by way of your accomplishments, your connections with high-placed individuals, or the size of your wallet, your car, or your home. When you are humble, you recognize that the sun and moon rise and set without your decree, that there are much larger forces at work than you can even imagine. An honest humility and quiet dignity are potent attractants. Faith follows the humble soul and finds therein a suitable soil in which to grow.

Be Ready to Reconsider

When we are beset by struggle, it's easy to fall back into the patterns, beliefs, and behaviors that got us there in the first place, even though this default position may no longer fit who we are becoming or where we are headed. Is it possible that your views about people and circumstances—even your own experiences—have been clouded or skewed by time and emotion? Might you be more enamored with your story than you are with getting at the truth? Take the time to review your life path with fresh eyes and have faith in the journey of self-discovery. Travel alone or with a skilled and compassionate guide. Perhaps you were not wronged in exactly the way you believe you were. Maybe you could reflect on the actions of yourself and others and shift your perspective on what happened. Look at things from different angles; put yourself in others' shoes. You may discover that taking a different vantage point opens up a world of possibilities you never realized could exist. In this new world, awareness and healing take the place of suffering and pain.

Be Hopeful

For the sake of us all, remain hopeful. Hope you can help create a world of peace in your lifetime. Hope that by the time the young ones are the leaders, greed and power will hold no sway. Raise your hopes and keep them alive and trust they'll never be shattered. In all things, set hopeful intentions and follow through with hopeful actions. Embrace a sense of promise and a deep yearning for a culture where prejudice can never stand—and encourage others to do the same. Fill your heart with the knowingness that we are all one earth family: people, rivers, animals, trees. When you walk your talk of acceptance and unity, hope that someone watches where your steps go. When you transform your thoughts of hope into unconditional service, hope the love in your eyes is noticed. Hope that the worst is over and the best is yet to be. Carry the light of hope in your words and deeds, and the wellspring of hope will never run dry.

Be Silent

Our days are filled with beeps and rings, buzzers and static, and conversations that are often more about filling up awkward silences than they are about authentic communication. Your spirit aches for a respite. First, accept the notion that silence offers much more than simply an absence of noise. When you enter silence, you enter into a virtual storehouse of inspiration and relaxation, rejuvenation and insight. In silence, fresh ideas may be hatched, questions answered, souls nourished. Within the quiet, you may access thoughts that are lost amid the usual, constant chatter. While absolute silence is nearly impossible to find, you can discover a hint of it in the rhythm of flowing water, in the whisper of a gentle wind, in a swollen sky before the rain and thunder sound their songs. You might call it meditation, prayer, time-out, or reflection. What matters is that you commit to brief or not-so-brief breaks away from the din of every day and allow yourself to be amazed and delighted by what you hear in the silence.

Be Challenged

Life may be marked by trials and hardship, yet challenges are the fertilizer that fosters growth. And, oh, what blossoms they can bring! The most demanding obstacles push you to explore new ways, forge alternative paths, and discover fresh solutions. Can you accept that today's challenge—no matter how unfair or insurmountable it seems—just might become tomorrow's gift? Every challenge you face asks you to summon up more of the good stuff in yourself and put it to the highest use you can muster. In fact, seeking to avoid challenge can rob you of opportunities to transform thorns into roses and sand into pearls. When you overcome challenges large and small, you chalk up a victory of spirit that tempers you with an interior strength and grace. Like the artist's chisel that releases an image from stone, challenge is a tool that invites you to use it for your own unfolding. Accept the invitation with gratitude and determination, and you will rise to meet every challenge.

Be Generous

Few things enliven the spirit more than giving. Even though you feel you have nothing to give, or you are starving to receive gifts of loving support and kindness yourself, find a way to give to another. Give more than you think you can. Give generously of your time or your money or the simple act of standing beside someone more alone and more in need than you. Ask: "Is there anything I can do for you?" Or skip the formalities and offer outright. Give anonymously if it makes it easier to give generously. Let your prayers be generous, your thoughts and words charitable and compassionate, and your presence comforting and dependable. When you do these things, you begin a flow of giving and receiving that cannot help but touch everyone in its path. Acts of generosity signify your faith that all will be provided. Whether you have $1 or $10 or $100,000, when you share generously, you demonstrate your trust that more of what you need will arrive when you need it. But in that moment, you revel in all that you have and you go beyond counting your blessings to sharing them freely in an abundance of soul-nurturing and faith-building ways.

Be Intentional

"Whatever" is not an inspired response to life's myriad choices. A healthy spirit has needs and desires and articulates them clearly. Granted, there is a fine line between intentionality and over-attachment to outcome, but you can learn to walk that line. Intentions set you squarely on the path toward creating what you want in life. Your intention may be to relocate to a more hospitable environment in which you can thrive, yet you may not know the exact town, city, or country where you want to live. Your intention may be to attain a greater state of physical well-being, yet whether you achieve that through mainstream or alternative methods is something you still need to discover. Intention lays the foundation; surrender fills in the blanks. For example, intention declares: "I am ready to bring greater outlets of creative expression into my life"; surrender waits with anticipation to see whether dancing, painting, singing, cooking, building, or writing beckons. Once you set your intentions clearly, you can go about your business filled with faith that the details will unfold in the appropriate manner at the perfect time.

Be Connected

Even the most solitary journey can benefit from connecting with others. These genuine connections are based primarily on how you feel when you're in each other's company, and they can provide a lifeline of protection and comfort. You know that when you call, you'll receive an answer. When you ask someone to sit with you while you vent or cry or say absolutely nothing at all, you know that someone will arrive at your door. Time with yourself is a precious commodity, yet time invested in creating mutually supportive connections with others carries even greater value. Healthy connections neither smother nor drain you. Solid connections are balanced, fair, and respectful. Authentic connections require that all parties be as truthful and present as they can be. Your connections grow and strengthen as you meet more people who, like you, seek the deeply heartfelt exchange that connecting can offer. The very best connections are fluid and flexible and able to move beyond conflict and blossom into friendships and partnerships filled with promise.

Be Adventurous

Do you believe that life offers an endless series of unexplored delights, or do you fear that every twist and turn forebodes dark and threatening danger? It's likely that your truth rests somewhere in between the two extremes. Living each day guided by a sense of limitless possibility emboldens you to stretch beyond your boundaries of the expected, known, and comfortable. When was the last time you struck up a conversation with a stranger? Took the train or bus instead of your car? Journeyed along a different path or road? It's natural to feel anxious, to be in a state of heightened awareness, when you venture beyond the familiar and contained. Yet how will you otherwise embrace newfound experiences? Consider heading into new emotional territory, opening up a new map of relationships, putting down your finger on an unknown landscape, and asking yourself, "Hmm, what if I stepped out onto this crowded byway or that solitary path and took a few steps with my heart and my eyes open?" There's only one way to find out, and it takes but a single step to begin a most excellent adventure.

Be Decisive

Your entire outlook is clearer, crisper, and less chaotic when you're decisive. Time spent wavering between this, that, and the other is time lost. Ungrounded wavering gums up the works and prevents you from moving ahead with purpose. Sometimes, the inability to come to a clear decision is nothing more than a strategy of avoidance. You avoid deciding so you can avoid committing. You avoid making a selection so you can avoid bringing an issue to completion. You can be of two minds or three or even four, but ultimately, you need to make up just the one. Once in a great while you may be called upon to make a life-changing decision, but most of the time, the choices in front of you are all good and hardly worth the mental and emotional turmoil you invest in them. Why trap yourself with an either-or choice when there are infinite shades of gray between the black and white? No matter what you choose, you take a step ahead and move from the murky and undefined to the lucid and straightforward. The choice is yours: decide what to do, and then do it.

Be a Blessing

You are a blessing to those around you. You need
not speak any particular words or cite any specific
writings or hold degrees or present special credentials.
When you take time to sit with someone who is
lonely, you are a blessing. When you send someone
off with good wishes, you bless their journey. When
you return a kind gesture with one of equal measure,
you offer up a blessing. No detailed ritual is required.
No songs need be sung. Your smile is a blessing.
Your very presence is a blessing. And when you
receive these same simple, uncluttered gifts graciously
from others, you offer up a blessing, too. Faith
enlarges your blessings—given and received—so
they grow and embrace all who are touched along
the way. When you openly express your gratitude
for the blessings that abound in your life, faith
expands for you and all who hear your expression.
If you are richly blessed—and of course you are—
you cannot help but share these blessings with
everyone you meet.

Be Trusting

Faith and trust are twins on the same road, walking hand in hand toward a shared destination. Neither is born out of facts, figures, and analysis, but they blossom when you listen to both your head and your heart and then make your way to somewhere in the middle. Trust that you are changing and growing and doing your very best and that others are doing the same. Trust that people will follow through, that their intentions are honorable, and that underneath the surface rests a genuine desire to do the right thing. Above all, trust your own instincts. Practice feeling your way through questions and sticky situations. When you have a problem to solve, check in with your body to see which solution brings you a sense of peace and which option causes your chest, stomach, or jaw to tighten. In your mind's eye, consider which picture portrays contentment and which one generates feelings of cloudy confusion. If something doesn't feel right or if another person does not seem trustworthy, depend on your feelings to guide you. They are telling you something important and are deserving of your highest trust.

Be Free

Though you are free to exercise personal choice and will, you may sometimes feel trapped by expectations and restrictions placed on you by inner or outer sources. Perhaps you are caught up in the opinions and projections of others, or you may be held back by a belief system you are not even aware of. Finding balance may be tricky: personal freedom invites you to respond to your inner promptings while also honoring the connections and commitments you have made. If you feel drawn to make changes in your job, home, social circle, or personal status, you are free to do so. You may solicit input from others, yet you are not beholden to follow their dictates. As a child, you may have found scant opportunity to exercise your free will and create a life of your own design. As an adult, you are a sovereign nation unto yourself. The map of your own becoming is etched upon your heart, and only you are endowed with the navigational tools to follow it.

Be Sustained

Faith is a powerful and enduring nutrient that can sustain you through times of great stress and grand elation. It provides the spiritual fuel to carry you through another hour, another day, and considerably longer. You must be prepared to keep up your end of the bargain, however. Faith is not a wonder drug that will magically wipe out your distress and instantly elevate your mood. You will come to find that faith casts a warm, even glow around your every step, not short-lived fireworks that promise much but deliver little. As you develop a consistent, measured approach to your deepening self-discovery, faith will help balance out rough and ragged edges, smooth highs and lows, and bring a comforting rhythm to your days. Faith is not merely something you delve into here and there, now and then, but a dependable practice that will support you over time and distance. When your confidence begins to fade and your determination dwindles, you can appeal to faith for sustenance and renewal.

Be Out of Control

You can neither control nor contain your world, so why even try? It's far better to adapt to constantly changing conditions and find strength in your ability to remain afloat. Given the natural order of things, your valiant attempts to manage and direct every detail of your life will ultimately prove futile. Even though things may settle now and then and you may reach a plateau, it is a foregone conclusion that things will shift again. You may, of course, dig your heels in and refuse to flow with the flux around you, but eventually you will find yourself out of synch with everything and everyone you encounter. Truly, what's the use? Your job is not—and never has been—to control your tiny corner of the universe. Instead, let go of your need to find boxes, pigeonholes, and spreadsheets for every aspect of your life, and learn to dance your way through a world that never stops moving and changing, no matter how hard you try to remain in control.

Be a Gardener

Growing your spirit is akin to growing a garden. You choose the seeds you wish to sow, selecting the hardy and long-lived. You prepare your soil by clearing away the rocks and debris that may have collected in your mind, spirit, or body. Then you plant in a most fertile soil, with gleeful anticipation and a prayer in your heart. Every seed you plant cries out for gentle tending. Each and every seedling of possibility—be it professional, artistic, spiritual, or personal—asks for time to take root, space to grow, and sun and rain to nourish its becoming. You wait. You tend. You weed out what doesn't belong, and then you wait some more. Have faith that the seeds you plant will blossom and bear fruit. Trust that the harvest will be bountiful, that your cornucopia will be filled with abundance, and that even as the seasons bring endings and barrenness, spring will appear once again and germinate the process anew.

Be Exactly Who You Are

Challenging times invite you to dig deep and stand tall. Advice and comments (sometimes unwanted) may fly at you from every direction. In these moments, it's all too easy to slip into someone else's version of who you should be. Instead, reinforce your commitment to be exactly who you are. Your way of engaging with life is not necessarily the way of your family, parents, children, or friends, so stay true to what matters for you. Have faith that even though others may misunderstand or criticize you, the one who knows you best is you. You may be softer and more vulnerable than you have let others see. You may possess a spiritual or religious devotion that even you have hidden from yourself. A profoundly practical, action-oriented side of you may have been kept under wraps for years. Now is the time to lovingly embrace every part of yourself and to trust deep within your heart that it is safe to come out of hiding. If those around you don't agree, find others who will fully and unquestionably honor and celebrate you exactly as you are.

Be Content

Contentment invites you to be at peace with the present. It's more subtle than happiness, more grounded than rapture, and accessible every moment. Contentment reassures you that you have enough and you are enough. When you're content, you rest in what is, instead of racing after what should be or could be. You're able to honor the here and now without regretting what might have been or fantasizing about what may come in the future. You still have dreams, but the difference is that they don't have you. Right now, are you content? Can you savor the apple in your hand, take delight in family and friends, and appreciate all that surrounds you without wondering if there's something better around the bend? Can you survey your world and feel the calm of contentment? Can you let yourself bask in what you have without reaching for more? Finding contentment doesn't mean that you settle for less or disregard your visions. Contentment simply asks you to accept that right now, given all that you have and don't have, you feel truly satisfied and serene.

Be Honest

There comes a time when you must be honest with yourself and others, no matter how hard that may be. Truth yearns to be acknowledged and embraced, and it offers you a quiet freedom when you give it the chance. If things have gotten to the point where you feel overwhelmed or paralyzed, tell someone trustworthy. If you could use a helping hand or shoulder to lean on, do not hesitate to say so. Find a willing ear that knows how to listen and to offer up assistance without judgment. When someone asks how you are, perhaps you can say, "Well, things are a bit rough right now." Perhaps you can admit that everything is changing and you're feeling somewhat shaky. You need not spill your guts or pour out your long, involved tales of drama and woe to everyone you see. More often than not, cracking the door to honesty just a bit will bring forth a surprisingly deep feeling of relief—not only to you, but to those who will step up and respond in kind to your heartfelt and genuine honesty.

Be Reverent

The world around you is teeming with the sacred. You need not travel to a distant land or pass under the archway of a designated holy site to find it. You can choose to experience a tender reverence within the most unlikely places. Notice the mother and daughter hugging tightly in the parking lot and feel their love radiating outward. Take a moment to stand in quiet admiration as the flag and all it symbolizes waves in the breeze. Turn your attention skyward as the sun dips below a multihued horizon. Yes, you can take a moment to step away from the crowd and sit beneath a tree that has offered up its shade for more than a hundred years. You can pull off the road and gaze upon a passing family of wild turkeys. You can marvel at the kaleidoscopic intricacies of a downtown building taking shape in a once-vacant lot. These quiet, unassuming expressions may not be labeled as sanctified or sublime—yet in their exalted presence we are called to reveal our highest regard and respect.

Be Solid, Be Strong

While it may seem that faith is all flowing and breezy and gentle, it also requires a rock-hard, unwavering devotion. This certainty may sound like an unreachable goal, but it is something to strive for. Think of yourself as rooted deeply, like the strongest tree, able to withstand powerful winds of change and raging storms. When life threatens to uproot you, remember that you carry within you the seeds for regrowth and new life. Hold steadfast to the knowledge that even if you are scattered here and there, broken or torn, you possess a core strength that will live on. Your inner light may flicker, but it does not disappear. When others try to pull you off your course of faith and into their whirlpool of desperation, summon up the strength to tell them, "Thank you, but that's not my way." Then turn in another direction and seek more supportive surroundings. When your faith is weakening, those who live by faith have a way of finding you and offering a much-needed dose of unconditional love while your own faith revives.

Be a Joyful Receiver

Joy is not only in the giving. The opposite side of the coin—receiving—offers equal reward. Receiving is not selfish, nor does it suggest you are greedy or self-serving. In fact, it matters not whether you are the giver or the receiver, but that the circle of reciprocity, of fair and unfettered exchange, is completed without reservation. When you deflect a compliment, a gift, or a kind gesture by insisting, "Oh, you shouldn't have," or by declaring, "Oh, I don't deserve or need or appreciate that," you stop the giver's intention in its tracks. The flow of giving slams up against the wall, and the circle remains incomplete. Why would you block another's inclination to celebrate and honor some aspect of who you are? There can be no joyful givers if no one joyously receives! When you graciously and gratefully receive, consider that you are giving the giver a most significant gift.

Be Filled with Faith

If you invite her along, faith can be a trusted companion on your personal journey. She has the capacity to carry you through uncharted waters and keep you on an even keel through storms that might otherwise tear you asunder. When the facts and figures just don't add up, insert faith into the equation. Trust that love will carry you through, though you don't have a clue how it will happen. Deepen your resolve even as you explore options and consider possibilities you can't yet see. Your walk of faith may look entirely different from anyone else's. It may be private and solitary, or you may discover faith within community. Trust that those around you are doing their very best in any given situation and if they could do better, they surely would. Have faith that the same holds true for you. After you lay down your need to understand, figure out, and predict every outcome, carry faith in your heart that everything happens for a reason. Then keep the faith that it's not always yours to know exactly what that reason may be.

Be Unafraid of Your Fears

Don't be surprised if you are beset by fears at the very same time you commit to living with faith. Fear shows up in a multitude of disguises. You will fear that you look foolish, that you are being led astray, that people are laughing at you. You might fear failure or success, change or stagnation. On some level, you may even fear creating a life of greater love and happiness. Anything that's new or unfamiliar or has the potential to transform your ways of being can bring up fear. However, fears usually live in your imagination and are not nearly as frightening as you think. When fear comes knocking, find the courage to crack open the door and recognize it for what it is. Say, "Oh, I know who you are," and send fear on its way. Sometimes fear will take a walk around the block and come right back and start knocking again. When it does, hold the line against your fears. Say, "No thanks, not interested," and send fear on its way once more. When fear knows you're no longer afraid, there's no reason for fear to return.

Be Whole

In a fragmented world, it's a challenge to be whole.
You're pulled in so many directions, your energy
scattered and bits and pieces flung hither and yon.
Sometimes it seems easier just to forget who you
really are and how much you are loved. Decide
instead to remember. Gather up the parts of yourself
that you've hidden away, and bring them back
into wholeness. Include your laughing self, your
crying self, your playful and serious or tender and
tough selves. Gather your faithful self, your
compassionate self, your courageous and vulnerable
selves. Round out your edges. Feel the difference
between reacting and responding, between holding
yourself accountable and offering yourself
compassion. When you leave parts of yourself in
the closet or on the shelf, the world isn't nearly as
rich as it's intended to be. Embrace a wide view
of your existence, and know that you are part of a
grand and glorious whole. When you do the math,
you'll understand: your whole is vastly greater
than the sum of your parts.

Be Clear

Clarity within begins with clarity in your surroundings. If you cannot get through the disarray in your home to find your keys, how will faith and hope find their way to the innermost rooms of your soul? If you constantly misplace important papers or arrive late for appointments, how can you possibly clear space for mindful self-reflection? In the same way that a new broom sweeps clean, you can clear your heart of old disappointments and unfinished business to prepare for new love to enter your life. Surely you can find one room or one corner or one shelf that radiates a scrupulous attention to detail and appreciation of simple beauty. Here, you might thoughtfully place a treasured picture or icon or an elegant element of nature that helps you focus and become quiet. When you return to these items, they will remind you to imbue your thoughts and actions with a crisp, sparkling quality that reflects a similar integrity and clarity within.

Believe

Faith asks you to believe in things you can't quite wrap your brain around. Do you truly believe that your situation can improve? Are you willing to believe that you can create more of your dreams and desires? Will you allow yourself to believe that no matter what the past has been, your future can be decidedly different? Believe that wonderful things are coming your way, and you are that much closer to creating them. Believe that unlimited support waits for you around every corner, and you are more likely to receive it. Don't be surprised when what you believe in your heart appears before your very eyes. And don't hesitate to believe it! Your visions and dreams are not simply make-believe. If you feel as though an angel has appeared in your path, why would you believe otherwise? Every day, in innumerable ways, your world adapts to reflect your beliefs. Believe that you deserve to be loved, to be valued, to be happy. When you let yourself believe in the power of faith, faith will believe in you.

Be Ecstatic

It may seem outlandish to think that you could reach a state of euphoric bliss and that you could be beside yourself with joy each and every day, but perhaps you could begin with something a bit less ambitious. Even when you feel weighed down with worry, you can invite lightheartedness to stop by for a visit. You can take a break from your concerns and seek out people or activities that make you giggle or even double over with laughter while tears roll down your cheeks. It's more than all right to set down your burdens now and then and find exquisite tickles of delight in small pleasures. Joy is where you find it. Elation requires little preparation and even less planning. Think of happiness as a lily, a rose, or other gorgeous flower whose only purpose is to bring enjoyment to your senses. In the same way, promise yourself to spread seeds of beauty wherever you can. Though you may feel surrounded by acres of barrenness, begin preparing your garden of delights today so that ecstasy and rapture can find you tomorrow.

Be Unattached to Outcome

When you have been encouraged to hold fast to your dreams, the idea of being unattached to the final outcome may seem downright contradictory. It's fine to set your sights on purchasing a new home, but if the sun rises and falls on owning that house in that neighborhood at that price and those terms, you've set yourself up for disappointment. If your every happiness revolves around a particular person giving you a particular gift in a particular setting, you trap yourself in a corner and limit your options. Why bother asking a question when you've already decided that only one answer could possibly be the right one? Releasing your control on how things turn out allows you to be surprised and delighted by a wide spectrum of experiences. Can you consider the possibility that an unexpected result might actually turn out to be better than what you had hoped for? Things are never all bad or all good, and letting go of your picture-perfect ideal is likely to offer you more opportunities for fulfillment and a deeper satisfaction far beyond what you had imagined.

Be the One

In every relationship, every work setting, and every community, there's a place uniquely suited for each individual. The key is to find the spot with your name on it and step into the shoes that only you can fill. You possess a set of qualities, skills, and talents found nowhere else in the whole of existence. When you are not in your true place, everything goes a bit flat and you may feel like a misfit. Are you the one who generates ideas and inspires others? Or are you the one who creates systems for the long haul? When the curtain goes up, are you working steadily behind the scenes or enthralling the audience from center stage? Do you bring truth and beauty, or tools and know-how? When you are exactly where you are meant to be, you will feel a solid sense of belonging and a quiet knowing. Your desires and visions will come to fruition with ease. And why shouldn't they? When faith and devotion lead you to your true spot, you will be one with a grand and infinite whole.

Be Able to Say "Yes"

How often has life offered you the opportunity to walk into new territory, but you turned down the invitation? Maybe fear got in your way or you slipped back into a default mode and felt unworthy, undeserving, or unprepared. There are times, of course, when the appropriate response is "No, thank you." The timing is off. Your focus is well placed elsewhere. Your instinct sends out a clear warning. However, if you're reacting from a place of resistance, "No" shuts down the flow of energy with a resounding thud. "Yes" opens gates and raises windows to bring in fresh air. "No" keeps you small and fearful. "Yes" expands your options and enlarges your worldview. Most often, being called to investigate new byways is an answer to a deeply held desire, spoken or not. You have been called because you are deserving, because you have manifested this very moment, and because you are uniquely qualified for the situation. A simple, yet hearty "Yes" can be the open sesame to new ways of being. The key is in your hand; don't drop it.

Be Grateful

Gratitude is so much more than uttering "Thank you" or sending off a quick note or e-mail. Those things are lovely and appreciated, but gratitude goes deeper and becomes a living part of who you are. Being grateful means practicing gratitude all the time—not just after the good things have come your way and your dreams have materialized. Try being grateful for the pain that teaches you a lesson about your body or the rain that changes your plans and treats you to a quiet, reflective day indoors. Able to make it out of bed and get dressed, albeit slowly? Be grateful. You-know-who still irritating you? Be grateful that you have people in your life, that you have feelings, and that you are able to feel. Cultivating gratitude takes time. At the beginning, tell yourself silently, "I am grateful for her," "I am grateful for this," and "I am grateful for every challenge that helps me to grow and become more at home with myself and others." In time, you will breathe gratitude in and out with a natural ease. And when that time comes, remember: be grateful.

Be a Listener

The voice of your own spirit is accessible to you and you alone, but only if you listen. When joy calls your name, will your grumblings and tired judgments drown out the music? Will a cacophony of old half-truths and deceptions prevent you from hearing truth's whisperings? What you "hear" may come to you in words, images, colors, feelings, or a fleeting sensation that you can't quite name. When you turn on the radio, gems of inspiration may reach out and touch you. If you lend an ear toward the night symphony or the melody of morning, you may glean a bit of insight or a well-placed nugget of wisdom. All too often, quiet murmurings are bubbling softly under the surface, thwarted by self-talk and meaningless conversation. The world has wonderful things to tell you, but you will never receive its messages if you choose never to listen. And if others wonder whether you've lost your head, tell them, "No, I'm just listening."

Be Inspired and Inspiring

When you fill yourself up with faith, you may be astounded at how others will respond to you. Even as you turn to uplifting art, music, books, service, and community for spiritual nourishment, your steps will enliven and inspire those around you. You won't need to do or explain a thing. You will emit a refreshing vibrancy, and without even trying, you will be noticed. Your circle of acquaintances will grow, as those who choose this path are attracted to each other much like birds singing the same song. You will radiate an inspiring energy that comes across as a breath of fresh air, and you will experience your own exhilaration when this vitality is reflected by others. By simply embodying greater degrees of faith and a newfound strength of spirit, you do your part to help transform the world. It's not your job to inspire others, but it just may become one of your greatest joys.

Be Slow

Your spirit knows no deadlines and answers no alarms. Your path to greater faith and inner wholeness is not designed to lead you to the finish line at top speed. Instead, slow and steady will carry you home. The choice is yours. You can attempt to race through every day, feet barely touching the ground beneath you, though you will not be sustained. Eventually, everything you're running from will catch up with you, and you will sink to the floor in exhaustion. Time is more flexible than the clock on the wall would have you believe. Wherever possible, inject more time into the process of life—rather than rushing hastily to churn out the end product. Just. Slow. Down. As you take steps to invite presence, forgiveness, inspiration, and appreciation more fully into your life, remember also to adjust your pace so they can join you on your journey. Unhurried progress allows a gradual ripening and graceful aging—and therein lies the sweetness of all things.

Be an Agent of Change

The days of waiting for a knight on a white horse to rescue you are over. The time for thinking that someone else will make things right, will reestablish peace and brotherly love, or will bring forth new ideals and ways of being is behind you. No matter how bad things appear, have faith that change is for the better—and that it begins with you. In small ways that may seem inconsequential, you hold the future in the palm of your hand. If you are a leader, now is your moment to lead. If you are a follower, your time also is now. If you believe your role is to obstruct and resist all that wishes to be born anew, your services are no longer needed. In this very instant, individuals and families and nations are changing the way they communicate, the way they live and love, and the way they create their destinies. When you find yourself complaining about who will fix everything that is wrong, remember: change is not a spectator sport; true and lasting change begins squarely with the woman or man you see in the mirror every day.

Be Forthright

Don't mince words when you have a mouthful to say. Why dabble in obfuscation and innuendo when the truth and the whole truth are aching to be spoken? Plainspoken sincerity need not be harsh or unkind; when you feel the truth rising up in you, harness its power. When you feel hurt or disrespected, it's appropriate to voice your emotion in a straightforward and heartfelt manner. When you feel that you or others have been treated unjustly, it is incumbent upon you to tell it like it is. When you swallow your truth and silence the power of your voice, you fan the flames of resentment and eventual bitterness. Your truth telling may not always reap the response you had hoped for, but if you remain unattached to any particular reaction, you will definitely garner a sense of well-being. Self-empowered individuals welcome the opportunity to express their truth candidly and never regret doing so. Truth serves no one until you muster up the courage to guide it with grace into the light of day.

Be Forgiving

Forgiving begins at home. Can you forgive yourself for saying what you said? For doing what you did? For not trusting your own instincts? For letting others sway you in directions you did not want to go? For trying to control other people's lives, all in the name of love? When you first offer forgiveness to yourself, you set into motion a rippling of forgiveness that spreads to everyone around you. It is not a quick, easy process. Forgiveness springs from a place that may be rarely visited; it may lie undiscovered and hidden. However, it is a journey worth taking. Forgiveness begins deep in your heart with a willingness to look beyond the actions that rest on the surface and to detach yourself just enough to see things in a different light. Then you may choose to travel even farther. Forgiveness brings peace, not so much to the forgiven, but always to the one who forgives. When you forgive yourself, you give yourself an invaluable gift. And for giving that gift, you receive immeasurable return.

Be Willing to Step Back

One of life's great paradoxes is how distance actually helps bring things closer together. When you're standing in the middle of a fast-running stream, it can feel like a torrential river. Everything is magnified—every twist and turn seems terrifying. In the same way, when you are embroiled in conflicts so large that they threaten to swallow up everyone involved, finding the peace and quiet of dry land seems impossible, too. Putting distance between you and the current can shift your perspective dramatically. During stressful times, when tempers may be short, step back, breathe, and maintain your distance. When you take a time-out, unexpected solutions may appear on the landscape. Boulders may suddenly turn into pebbles. What seem like mountains may revert to their actual size. Harsh words and hurt feelings may no longer darken the sky. Sometimes, stepping back is the very first step in moving forward.

Be

Although the message is frequently lost in the hubbub of daily life, who you are is infinitely more important than what you do. You can spend time listening to a friend's problems, but if you don't choose to be present, you're not doing anyone any favors. You can try your hardest to convince someone of your feelings, but if you don't choose to be honest, your words are meaningless. Are you so busy giving to others that you never allow yourself to receive all that they offer? Are you willing to be vulnerable instead of defensive? Can you let go of the need to figure out everything, fix problems immediately, and barrel your way through to a predetermined set of answers? Sometimes the best course of action is simply to be. Ultimately, you choose. You can be patient and contemplative, or manipulative and frazzled. You can be like a river and flow, or you can try with all your might to swim against the tide. Eventually, everything comes to completion. There are many pathways to well-being. First, you must let yourself be.

Beckon

Faith helps you gently bring forth that which you desire most. Beckoning is a far cry from going out and making things happen with a forceful hand. To beckon means to quietly hold out the palm of your hand while a baby chick decides whether she wants to come closer. To beckon is to do your homework, lay the groundwork, then sit and wait quietly without yelling or manipulating or demanding anything of anyone. Take time in your day for silence, and you beckon fresh insight and calm. Take your shoes off and move about the room, and you beckon dancing. Think loving thoughts and let judgment fall away, and you beckon the opening heart. With faith at your side, there's no need to prod or to try every which way to engineer an outcome. Grace beckons love. Truth beckons greater understanding. Clarity beckons forward movement. Beckoning whispers yet does not shout, gestures yet neither pushes nor pulls. No matter how daunting your challenge, your most powerful first step is to beckon.

Be Uplifted

Does the weight of daily life pull you down and hold you fast like glue on the basement floor? Do you feel as though the tide threatens to take you under for the third time—despite your valiant attempts to keep your head above water? When others' negativity or judgment threatens to drag you down, you can choose to be raised up. Above the muck and mire, you can continue to embrace and radiate feelings of acceptance, goodwill, and kindness. To do this, you might imagine a soft, yet potent breeze lifting you up or strong arms reaching to boost you to a higher plane. You may surround yourself with truly beautiful images or sounds, connect with your personal source of love, or recall a sweet and lovely memory that lives in your heart. You need not go along with others who wallow in misery, despair, or perpetual unhappiness. You have the ability to access whatever helps you rise above the petty and mundane, and when you do, you will be uplifted.

Be Resilient

If you have the courage to delve deeply into life, you will stumble now and again. When you least expect it, when you're feeling invincible, you will miss the mark. You will glide over some of your highest hurdles and trip and fall when faced with others. Don't let that stop you. What's important is that you get back up again, dust yourself off, take a deep breath, and get back in the saddle. No matter what anyone else may think or say, you possess what it takes to overcome every adversity thrown your way. Granted, you may not always suffer your indignities with grace. You may not always recover as quickly as you would like. But simply giving up is not an option. Your spirit is hardy and robust, and even when you feel as frail as the wings of a butterfly, you have within you an irrepressible urge to flourish. You can and will rebound—more vigorous and resolute than ever.

Be Awestruck

Although it isn't always easy, the toughest times require you to believe in the greatest, grandest possibilities. Can you allow yourself to be brought to your knees by miracles and finely orchestrated "coincidences" that defy rational thought? Can you soften your gaze and recognize the truly extraordinary when it happens right in front of you? If you think small, if you believe that your own mind contains every single potential outcome, you may miss an infinite universe of possible scenarios. Are you willing to see the unseen at work, to marvel at how your simplest steps can lead to unimaginable conclusions? Can you sufficiently chip away your armor and swoon at the unmistakable awe that exists just inches outside your usual concerns? Untold beauty and inexplicable synchronicities are at work in every moment. When we toss aside our rigid pictures of how things are supposed to occur, we acknowledge the grandeur of how they actually do. And only then can we reclaim the true meaning of the word "awesome" and the vastness and beauty of all that it contains.

Be Curious

Faith invites you to view your world as a place of untold wonder and endless curiosity. What lies beyond that gate? How does that machine work? What makes her tick? Who's really behind that perfect façade? It's worth asking questions, quietly or out loud. What fuels your drive, motivates your desires? Which of your relationships are born out of healthy attachment and which rest on co-dependency or dysfunction? Is there more to living than work, home, keeping up with the Joneses—and if so, what might it possibly be? Is there a community or chosen family in which you feel safe, comfortable, and at home—and if so, when will you join them? Is there some kind of force, being, or energy larger than you—and if so, what do you call it and how do you approach and explore it? What is the nature of Earth, and how do you come to terms with the vast beauty, breadth, and diversity of its inhabitants? Curiosity does not require that you run to the library to find every answer, only that you remain inquisitive and interested and, most assuredly, intrigued by every question.

Be Prepared to Surrender

The day will come when you are no longer satisfied to read about faith, think about faith, or analyze and attempt to understand the definition or rationale of faith. You will hunger for a more palpable experience and will want to feel faith working through your body and in your life. It's nothing you can plan or strategize; you will simply be ready to surrender. Surrender is not a giving up, but rather it is a purposeful act of getting out of your own way and yielding to something beyond the capacity of your intellect. When you're prepared to surrender to the power of faith, you'll no longer view yourself as the captain of the ship—and you'll be content to buckle up and go along for the ride. You'll stop trying to figure out everything, orchestrate every move, and micromanage to the nth degree. Instead, you'll wait as long as it takes for things to unfold. You'll take heart in every consequence and trust every truth that emerges along the way. And you'll graciously accept the rightness of every end result without judgment.

Be Bold

Quiet faith requires a significant degree of boldness. You must have courage to believe in nudgings of the spirit that you can't always explain and outcomes that may at first be invisible to the naked eye. There are inner and outer battles to be fought, and you may feel yourself drawing a sword to cut through doubts and entanglements that bind you. At times, it will require every ounce of courage you have to stand up for what you know is true and good and right. Your courage will arise from the heart and travel through you with a mighty force you may never have known. In response, you may take greater risks and conquer heights once thought insurmountable. You may feel more vulnerable at the very same moment you are emboldened by a burgeoning sense of protection. Faith is for the willing and also for the bold. Together, your willingness to be bold can infuse your faith to new heights and support you through times that illuminate and test your most vulnerable weaknesses.

Be Effervescent

Not all of us are sparkly and bubbly—and certainly not during difficult times—but that doesn't mean we must walk around like a sack of soggy potatoes. There is surely something that brings a smile to your face, a twinkle to your eye, a glimmer of something spirited and alive. Could you make it your goal, your intention, to uncork at least some of these bottled-up feelings and emit a bit of the bubbly each day? And if that feels outside your reach, might you devote yourself to exploring the deeper reasons behind your lack of enthusiasm for living? Even when all around you seems to be crumbling, what might it take for you to find a bit of cheer in someone else's buoyant walk, in the sights and sounds of nature, or in the enjoyment of a book or movie? Rather than attempt to put on a happy face, why not ask faith to help you reach inside and find the sparkle buried beneath the blahs? No matter how long your effervescence has been away, it is not gone; you can still retrieve and reclaim it.

Be Unlimited

Developing faith, trust, compassion, and presence is deep core work. You will be called upon to exercise a great deal of self-determination and to search the inner recesses of your soul. Daunting as it seems, if you are reading these words, you are up for the task. Along the way, you will stumble upon fundamental truths. You will recognize that your potential is limitless and that you have a bottomless supply of resources at hand. You will come to know that you are never alone, that you exist within a boundless universe, and that you possess an innate ability to erase hardship and struggle from your life. You were created from a blueprint that rests upon unconditional love and that values prosperity over lack. Even as you may slip and fall, the seed inside you remains potent and capable of bringing forth the fruits of an expanded life. You begin by peeling away the layers that have hardened your heart and opening yourself up to the infinite treasures that lay nestled within.

Be Disillusioned

Your faith walk is not a high-speed blast down an interstate highway marked by brightly illuminated exit ramps and well-placed signage. There will be detours, temporary and permanent closures, and unanticipated blockages. You may feel unsure of where you're going and why. You may question the entire idea and feel strongly inclined to go back to where you came from. Your strength and conviction will suddenly begin to melt away, and you will feel naked, alone, and lost. "What a crock!" you may think. That's okay. In fact, it's to be expected. At some point, you will become disillusioned and perhaps feel that you have been the target of a rude cosmic joke. This is the very time to push on, to regain your bearings and correct your course. Pause and review where your trust has taken you thus far, how your heart swells when you feel in synch with a greater ideal, which new people have appeared in your life, and how you have given and received new levels of happiness and fulfillment. Growing disillusionment is no reason to stop. On the contrary, it reflects a powerful incentive to keep moving forward, plus a strong directive to "yield."

Be Authentic

No matter how labyrinthine your journey of personal growth and discovery, it always leads directly back to you. The intention is not to change you into someone else, but to strip away false fronts so you can discover, recover, and uncover your genuine essence. Continuing to wear masks that hide your true feelings or to live a life predicated on something other than your unadulterated truth hinders the process and upends the natural order. Attempting to recreate yourself to look like, dress like, or live like a high-profile celebrity or anyone else is a slap in the face of whoever or whatever you consider to be the source of your existence. The more authentic you are, the simpler life can be. Why invest energy in creating and maintaining unnatural images and playing insincere roles when you could be reinvesting in your most precious and valuable resource? Being authentic is being yourself, your whole self, and nothing but yourself, thereby giving the world the priceless and irreplaceable treasure that is you.

Be Abundant

It's all too easy to live in scarcity, believing that you deserve little and feeling satisfied with a bit here and a scrap there. Could you possibly open your eyes wide enough to see a life overflowing with prosperity? Can you imagine that you have the opportunity to be showered with health and happiness, the sincere love of family and friends, deeply nourishing work, and a heaping helping of comfort? Too often, the issue is not that we ask for or expect too much, but that we are willing to accept so very little. Setting your sights higher, conceiving of a grander, more fulfilling existence, is neither unreasonable nor self-serving. Regardless of your past, you have every right to walk confidently toward a gloriously abundant future. Yet if you continue to play small, to be satisfied with barely enough, you may never know the exhilaration that comes with a truly abundant life. Faith and determination will help you leap to higher levels, but only you can set the height of the bar.

Be Incomplete

As soon as you believe that you're "done"—that you're as kind, loving, healed, and whole as you can ever be—you might as well stop breathing. You are a singular work in progress, always evolving and forever expanding. Perhaps you've reached the top of your game in your professional life, but you still have some work to do cleaning up old emotional wounds. Maybe you are a kind, trustworthy, and generous friend, always jumping in to help another, yet less proactive when it comes to self-nurturance. No matter what your physical or educational or economic limitations, you can always choose to refine some aspect of your personal development. Don't be too hasty to declare yourself at the edge of your limits. Carry the faith that, for now, you are perfect in your imperfection. And know that as soon as you perfect one aspect of yourself, you will temporarily land in a place of perfect imperfection again. Someone may ask, "How are you?" and when you respond, "Everything's perfect," you can take comfort in knowing you speak your highest truth.

Be a Beacon

It matters not whether you are rich, famous, important, or powerful. Others are watching you in the best possible kind of way. Perhaps you know them; perhaps you don't. It may be a child—yours or someone else's. It may be someone you will never meet. They're watching where your steps go. They're listening to your words, observing how you regard others who are like you and unlike you. Imagine the impact you might have on a stranger who crosses your path at work, school, or play—simply by demonstrating a bit of kindness or a glimmer of hope. This is not about putting on a show or acting a certain way to get attention. This is about remembering that all your words, thoughts, and actions carry great power and potential, and you can choose to be a beacon who lights the way for others in a quiet and unassuming manner. There's no magic switch that you turn on and off. It's an inner light that radiates from within you and can be felt by others. And without your even trying, its warmth can change the world.

Be an Achiever

Coupled with common sense, faith can catapult you into new levels of achievement. Yet what does it mean to achieve? Too often, we look at high achievers as those who have reached the pinnacle of success in their chosen fields. We seek out awards and prizes, wealth and power, as the hallmarks of such success. Setting realistic aspirations for your circumstances is one way to approach your personal potential; another is to extend your reach far beyond the level you've been led to believe is rightfully yours. Why not dream and manifest a life lived large? Why not broaden your concept of what it means to be successful? Your greatest achievements may occur in the realm of your spiritual development or self-actualization. Your highest accomplishments may revolve around your ability to form and maintain rich, full-bodied relationships grounded in mutual acceptance and unconditional love. When your ambition and inner courage foster a life marked by compassion, peace, generosity, and service, you have attained one of the greatest achievements most only dare to hope for.

Be a Ripple in the Pond

When your soul is filled with joy or simple contentment, pass it along. When you have exhilarating news, share it with others. When you are inspired by the good deeds of another, go out and inspire someone with your own good deeds. If you have healed yourself through prayer, spread the news. If you have found inner peace through forgiveness or meditation or morning walks, let others in on your secret. Even the smallest undertaking can ripple out and multiply in astounding scope and potency. A small group of people with shared interests can rouse millions to action and create a groundswell of positive change. Toss a small measure of compassion, a crumb of appreciation, or a nibble of gratitude into your world. Know that in your small way, your intentions will ripple out and touch kindred souls who will, in turn, create their own ripples—and so on and so on, until the world is awash in waves of human kindness and infinite delight.

Be Called

Once you learn to listen, you will eventually be called. You may or may not hear your name, yet you will know unmistakably that you have been chosen for something for you and you alone. It may be a new job opportunity, a volunteer position, travel, or relocation. Your first thought may be, "Uh-oh, be careful what you wish for." You will hesitate to answer and will most likely make excuses or altogether disbelieve what is happening. The call will come at the worst possible time and will quickly reveal itself as impractical, inconvenient, and wholly ridiculous. However, you will know that this is one call you cannot forward to your voice mail. If you have invited faith into your life, nurtured your relationship with faith, and embraced your faith in earnest, you will answer the call. You will at once let go of people, places, and circumstances that you love, and with faith beside you, you will step forward with courage into a brave new beginning... all because you made the choice to be filled with faith.

Be Brilliant

You have within you an inextinguishable brilliance that can illuminate the world. It may lie beneath the surface, hidden under old wounds and traumas that did their best to snuff out your radiance. But they did not succeed. It is time to throw back the curtains and meet up with the light of day. Your brilliance may have flickered and even sputtered, but this spark, planted deeply at the core of who you are, has never gone out and is now ready to be rekindled. Whether you knew it or not, faith remained at your side as you wended your way through the darkness and conquered your fears. Your unrestrained willingness to step into a brighter future, buoyed by your resilience and unwavering devotion to your own becoming, sustained you along the journey. It is safe to show the fullness of your light and to share your radiance with all you meet. The road stretches out before you, and with faith as your loyal companion, your brilliance will guide your steps and light the way.

Be at Peace

Faith beckons. In her calm and gentle way, she invites you to be strong and courageous and willing to surrender your hold on all things. She asks you to be trusting, to be grateful, and to be ready to reconsider some of your longest-held beliefs. Should you accept her invitation, you just may find yourself enjoying more authentic balance in your life along with a lasting peace. The constant chatter in your mind will quiet down; the endless guessing and second-guessing may come to an end. You will make choices that nourish and raise your spirits, and you will seek out others who share your hunger for a positive and prosperous way of living. In time, as you build your spiritual muscle, you will foster a measure of comfort amidst the sometimes harsh world you inhabit. As you do, a new tranquility will tiptoe into the spaces around your heart. Here, you will possess a wellspring of serenity to draw from whenever you choose. And here, together with faith, you will be at peace.

About the Author

Rachel Snyder loves words, loves people, and loves assisting women and men to live full-spectrum lives. She is the author of the popular book *365 Words of Well-Being for Women* (also released as *Words of Wisdom for Women*), which has been read and enjoyed by women, mothers, and countless others around the world. For decades, she has inspired, entertained, and educated people through her books, greeting cards, columns, poetry, and personal appearances. She offers up her unique brand of "intelligent inspiration" at www.rachelsnyder.wordpress.com.